The Kiss of a Hummingbird's Wing

Written by Jenny Feely

Illustrated by Stephen Axelsen

Flying Start
to Literacy®

Contents

Chapter I:
An impossible wish

Julio was excited. The hummingbirds were coming, and he wanted to see them. But more than anything, he wanted to be kissed by a hummingbird's wing.

Julio's mother had been kissed by a hummingbird's wing, so had his father and his little sister – and she was only three.

Everyone said that seeing a hummingbird up close and feeling its wing on your cheek were the most wonderful things that had ever happened to them.

The only way to get kissed by
a hummingbird's wing was to put on
a hummingbird helmet-feeder and stand
very, very still.

Standing very, very still was impossible
for Julio. It was something he had never,
ever done. He was always running around.
Even when he was asleep, he rolled around
all night.

Chapter 2:
No help in sight

"Don't worry," said Julio's father as he cleaned out the bird feeders. "I was just like you when I was young. I was always running around."

Dad filled the bird feeders with the sugar syrup that the hummingbirds liked to eat.

"How did you learn to stay still?"
asked Julio, jumping up and down.

"I just grew out of it," said Dad.

"You are a clever boy," said his mother. "You will find a way to stand still when the hummingbirds arrive."

"I will?" asked Julio, as he hopped from one foot to the other.

"You know, you remind me of a hummingbird," said his mother.

"How?" asked Julio.

"You're full of energy like a hummingbird. Maybe you need to think like a hummingbird."

Julio rolled his eyes. *How was he supposed to think like a bird?*

But it was all he had to work on, so Julio decided to try out his mother's idea.

Chapter 3:
Think like a hummingbird

"If I am going to think like a hummingbird, first I have to find out about them," said Julio.

To his great surprise, he discovered that hummingbirds use lots of energy, just like he did. They flap their wings so fast that all you can see is a blur. They use lots of energy to stop in the air and stay in the one place.

But Julio still didn't know how to think like a hummingbird. He was about to give up, when he had an idea.

"If I can't think like a hummingbird, perhaps I can act like one," he said.

Julio flapped his arms as fast as he could and raced around the garden to all the flowers that hummingbirds liked so much.

He flew sideways
and forwards
and backwards.
He even tried to fly upside down –
just like a hummingbird!

The more he flapped his arms and ran
around the garden, the more he felt like
a hummingbird.

Soon, he was exhausted. He leaned against
the wall where he stayed still for a very,
very long time.

When Julio's mother saw him standing as still as a rock, she said, "That's it! That's exactly what you have to do. Tomorrow, when the hummingbirds come, you just have to think like a hummingbird."

"No," Julio said. "I don't have to **think** like a hummingbird. I have to **act** like a hummingbird."

Chapter 4:

Act like a hummingbird

The next morning, Julio jumped out of bed.

"Today is the day," he shouted, as he skipped down the stairs.

"I'm going to do it," he yelled, as he hopped around the kitchen. "I'm going to be kissed by a hummingbird's wing!"

Everyone went into the garden and put on their helmets. They stood very still and waited for the hummingbirds.

All except Julio. He planned to fly all around the garden. Then, when he was exhausted, he would put on his helmet and stand very still.

Suddenly, a gentle humming sound filled the garden. Julio didn't have time to race around until he was exhausted.

The hummingbirds were here, and he was jiggling and jumping and hopping and spinning. He couldn't stop.

"Stand still," said his father.

"Stop jiggling," said his mother.
"You'll scare away the hummingbirds."

"I can't keep still," said Julio.

"You did it yesterday," his mother said.
"If you did it then, you can do it now.
Act like a hummingbird!"

21

Julio put on his helmet and closed his eyes. He tried to remember what he had done yesterday – how he had run around the garden and flapped his arms very, very fast. He remembered how tired he had felt when he stopped and how good it was to rest.

Julio let his arms hang loose at his sides.

And that is when it happened. There was a humming next to his ear, and he felt a breeze brushing his face. Then he felt the tiniest tickle right on his cheek.

It was a kiss from a hummingbird's wing. It was the most wonderful thing that had ever happened to him.

A note from the author

I have never seen a hummingbird up close in real life, but I would love to. They are amazing animals – they are so small and so fast. When I came across a picture of people with hummingbird feeder hats, it made me imagine what it would be like to be that close to a hummingbird.

I've had butterflies land on me and their touch felt like a light kiss. I think a hummingbird next to my face would feel much the same. But I'm not very good at staying still, and this is where I got the idea for this story.